PSYCHIC DEBRIS, CROWDED CLOSETS:

The Relationship between the Stuff in Your Head and What's Under Your Bed

2ND EDITION

introducing the on-line community
Clear Just 10 Then Do It Again

REGINA F. LARK, PH.D., CPO®

For information: regina@aclearpath.net

ISBN: 978-1500455590

Cover by Barbara Gottlieb
www.gottgraphix.com

Published in Partnership with
Purple Distinctions Self Publishing
www.purpledistinctions.com
Venture, CA 93004

Printed in the United States of America

PSYCHIC DEBRIS, CROWDED CLOSETS:

The Relationship between the Stuff in Your Head and What's Under Your Bed

2nd Edition

introducing the on-line community
Clear Just 10 Then Do It Again

Join our email list to receive the latest de-clutter tips and updates. Go to aclearpath.net or scan our QRcode with your smart phone.

To my chronically disorganized clients:

For all that you teach me, I thank you from my heart. Remember: You are not your stuff; your stuff is not you.

TABLE OF CONTENTS

ACKNOWLEDGEMENTS
FROM THE FIRST EDITION

Two terms are used interchangeably through this book: *psychic debris* and *head trash*. The first time I heard the term *psychic debris* was at the Agape International Spiritual Center in Culver City, CA. Reverend Michael Beckwith described how the negativity of psychic debris keeps us from finding our path. Ann Connor, business coach extraordinaire, introduced me to the concept of *head trash*. Starting out as a business owner and entrepreneur was scary, but Ann helped me put my new journey into perspective.

In my work as a professional organizer I witness first-hand the crushing weight of negative thinking on the lives of some of the kindest, smartest, and most cluttered people with whom I have had the privilege of working with.

My mother has given me the opportunity to work with her on her own de-cluttering projects, and I thank her for that. She's a talented, intelligent, and all-around awesome woman, and I appreciate her many gifts. My dad, a clinical psychologist, has offered me valuable insight about some of the challenges my clients may be facing in the process of uncovering, discarding, and discovering the stuff beneath the surface.

Three people helped me to bring this manuscript to life. I'm grateful to the amazing Antoinette 'Toni' Dee who edited the first draft and works with me at A Clear Path in the official capacity of Director of Operations and Outreach.

Barbara Gottlieb designed and maintains my website, created all of my marketing and printed materials, and created this book cover. Barb, your support and your ideas keep me competitive and looking really good. And Ronni Sanlo – my BFF, Palie, kindred spirit - I could not be in the hands of a better editor and publisher. There are no words.

Regina F. Lark,
Los Angeles, California
January 2013

ACKNOWLEDGEMENTS
FOR THE 2ND EDITION

After the launch of the first edition of *Psychic Debris* two wonderful things happened. I completed a Master's level training program which earned for me the designation of Certified Professional Organizer in Chronic Disorganization through the Institute for Challenging Disorganization (ICD - www.challengingdisorganization.org). I'm inspired by the Institute's commitment to research and collaboration with the mental health community, and my work as a professional organizer is enhanced as a result of my ICD education

In addition to my education, I had the good fortune to hire Kimberly Zanetti Purcell, my right-hand woman in all things connected to A Clear Path. Kimberly's intelligence, positivity, and support have no boundaries. A great deal of my current success - as an organizer, author, and business owner - has much to do with her oversight and dedication to the work that we do.

Regina F. Lark,
Los Angeles, California
Summer 2014

PSYCHIC DEBRIS, CROWDED CLOSETS:

2nd Edition

Introduction to the 2ⁿᵈ Edition

In the year since *Psychic Debris* was first published I enrolled in an 18-month, master's level program to become a student of, then a subject-matter expert, on Chronic Disorganization (CD).

According to Judith Kolberg, co-founder of the Institute for Challenging Disorganization (ICD, formerly National Study Group for Chronic Disorganization), chronic disorganization has three components: 1) the persistence of severe disorganization over a long period of time; 2) a daily undermining of one's quality of life by disorganization; 3) a history of failed self-help efforts.

My work in this area of chronic (and challenging!) disorganization means that I get to explain to my clients and audiences that a big reason for their clutter has more to do with the hardwiring of their brain than anything else. I have walked into countless homes where I hear these and similar sentiments by people describing the clutter and ensuing chaos that clutter may bring:

- I clean and clear but it always comes back;
- I don't know how it got this way;
- I must be really lazy;
- It's been this way all my life;
- I have a dozen organizing books but nothing seems to work;
- My mother and sister are just like me.

My training in CD has made me hyper-aware of my clients' lives *after* I leave each home. In order to ensure that we work toward maintaining their cleared spaces, we have to talk about shifting those very habits that ensure the clutter and chaos will return.

What I now know is this: in order to keep clutter at bay, two things have to happen. First, change (or shift) the habits and behaviors that allow the clutter to thrive. Second, develop a new and better relationship to space and stuff.

The 2nd edition of *Psychic Debris* retains the initial messages - change your thinking and your relationship to clutter, and maintain your de-cluttered spaces with new tools and ideas. Included in the new edition is a chapter that explores more fully the challenges of chronic disorganization. The 2nd edition also introduces you to Ms. Max Wong, the inspiration for our new Facebook community which we call *Clear Just 10, Then do it Again!*
(https://www.facebook.com/groups/clearjust10/?ref=br_tf)

By the time you finish this book, I hope you are so excited to start your de-clutter projects that you join *Clear Just 10.* You may share your space-clearing stories, upload photos of your stuff heading to a donation center, and encourage and support members of the *Clear Just 10* community as they deal with their own clutter issues.

INTRODUCTION
FROM THE 1ST EDITION

I'm a professional organizer. I help people clear the clutter that surrounds them so that they feel better not only about their spaces but also about their lives. When I started this business, I truly thought I was just going to do garages, closets, drawers, and underneath sinks. As I moved deeper into this work, I began to see the relationship between how people talked about their lives and how they described what was or was not happening with them. I would look around their spaces as I listened to how they were describing what they thought about their things. I heard how people talked about feeling stuck in their lives as I opened their closet doors. Things would literally fall down on me! It was an interesting way to strategically see how people thought about who they are, how they walk through their day, and indeed, their own relationship with self. I realized that clutter – and de-cluttering – is all about relationships!

We have many personal goals and some professional ones. As we start moving through the work of de-cluttering our spaces, we may find ourselves tapping into our body, mind, and spirit. There is a strong interconnectedness between how people *walk* through their lives, how they *think* about their lives, and what their connection is to the things that surround them. When we're not feeling right with ourselves, when we're feeling as if we're stepping into chaos, every step has a huge impact on how we're going to walk through our day.

Psychic Debris, Crowded Closets is about how the stuff in our head and what's under our bed crowd us and how we feel hamstrung by them. So however you define clutter and however you define ways that you're not able to move forward, this book is for you.

Let's begin this journey together.

SENSE OF SELF: MEDIA AND HEAD TRASH

Our brain can be a powerful tool or a staggering enemy. It can uplift and elevate how you think about things just as easily as it can disparage and deny the goodness that's around you. We tend to wear negative thinking as protective armor, shielding us from doing the important work of transforming how we think about who we are and how we manage. It's as if our brain abandons us to our clutter.

One of the most important and most profound statements I've learned is this:

The only thing over which I have control in my life, in the universe, on the planet, in both my personal and professional relationships, is how I think about those relationships.

My mind is so powerful! It allows me to elevate or denigrate Regina or the people around me at any given moment. I was looking in the mirror one day after showering. You know how you get out of the shower and stand in front of a mirror and pick yourself apart? I can do that with the best of 'em! I was staring at the new age spot on my face, the one near the new line on my left ear lobe. I was so critical! Everything about me looked old. I wondered, *Why can't I just look at myself and say, 'Wow, nice shoulders, Regina,'* and move on? Why does the negative hit me quicker than anything else? And then I began to listen, to really hear, every single word that came out of my mouth when I would describe my life. I needed – and had the power – to change how I thought about myself. When I look at the Regina in the mirror, I need to look at the good things, the positive things, about myself.

I really believe we're conditioned from the moment we leave the womb to feel that there's something wrong with us, and later, to think it, especially when we're bombarded with media ads on television, on billboards, and in the magazines we read which promote perfectionism. So we end up surrounding ourselves with the things that are supposed to make us feel better. We are actually subjected to over three thousand messages a day telling us that there's something wrong with us, that there's a product that can make it all better.

I do a lot of networking and often come across people selling anti-aging products, as if we could stop this process. Constant negative messages surround us both socially and culturally. Your subconscious mind believes every single thing you tell it about yourself. As a result, this negative thinking, the way in which we continually criticize ourselves, is absorbed by your brain and then owned by your sub-conscious. There is a huge connection between the internal baggage of negative thinking and the external baggage of having more than you need. I will explain further and break this down for you.

These negative ideas are what I call *psychic debris* or *head trash*. They're terms I use to describe the stuff in my head that tells me that I can't do something, that X is not going to happen, that I'm too much of this, not enough of that, too old, too fat, that I don't have enough education, blah, blah, blah! We're constantly filling our heads with trash, with

really negative images about how we are perceiving ourselves. I'm here to tell you from personal experience: you
begin to believe this stuff!

I started my organizing business in 2008. I'd never started a
business before. After all, I have an academic background
and worked on college campuses. *Somebody* at some college or university always signed my paycheck. But one
day, after a fairly contentious period of time, I was laid off
from my position as a director at UCLA Extension. I understand now that it really wasn't the right job for me and I
had been trying to get out of it for several months before I
was actually laid off. Oh how the Universe works!

The day I was laid off, I felt so thankful, so free, and yet it
was the first time in my life that I didn't have the next thing
to go to. What was I going to do? I have long been a posi-
tive-thinking person so there was no doubt in my mind that
whatever I was going to come upon, whatever I was going
to land on, I was going to be a success. There was no other
option. But I had to create a depth of intentional positive
thinking that I could draw upon with every breath, every
moment, every single day.

I had to define for myself what success is. I started working
with a business coach. Some negative stuff had been creep-
ing into into my language, such as "I don't know how to do
that. How do you market that? I don't understand how to
write a business plan." My business coach started telling
me how the head trash was going to bring me down. Even
though I have a very positive outlook on the one hand, I
had these annoying doubts about what I could and could
not do on the other hand. So I changed my language about

it. I became attentive to every single word that left my mouth. Truly. For example, I don't walk into a room filled with women and say, "Hey you guys." Guys? Hardly! Every word that came from my mouth was intentional and the head trash began to ebb away.

Assignment:

Describe some of the head trash that you feed yourself. What comes up for you? What do you tell yourself you *can't* do as you are walking through your day? What head trash is resonating with you?

I'm not good enough

I can't do "X"

I'll never be able to do "X"

REDEFINING SUCCESS

I had to redefine the word *success*. In our culture, success usually means X number of dollars in the bank or a particular kind of intimate relationship or children who are valedictorians. Whatever it is, we have very culturally-prescribed ideas about what success is. When I started my business, I had very little money so I had to really understand and define what success means for Regina. I came to the conclusion that, for me, success meant I didn't have to borrow money from my father. (So far, in my nearly six years of business, I haven't needed to borrow from him. I feel like a huge success!) I wake up feeling like a successful person everyday because I decided my own definition of success, even though it was not a culturally inscribed definition. In order to get away from the head trash, I had to create my own definition about what is good, what is right, what is successful for my business and for myself.

I hear people talk about being lazy, about feeling that they can't do "it" right, whatever they define as "it." I hear people feeling overwhelmed, overextended, procrastinating, feeling so overwhelmed that it's hard to move forward. You're going to believe your negative words if you keep telling yourself these things. I know that it's not easy to make the switch, but I want you to believe that you can do it. Go for the uplifting and elevating words, the positive words.

Now that you've started writing down your head trash, I want you to look at it even deeper. Expand the list you made earlier. Brainstorm with yourself. Look around.

When you're sitting in a comfortable space, get your pen and paper or iPad and list your head trash. What is it that you tell yourself? Be honest. You may even ask people whose opinions you trust. (This may cause you to feel vulnerable. If that's an uncomfortable place, don't go there.)

As time progresses, keep your list with you and start making hash marks next to a head-trash item every time you think or say it, every time they start hitting your head, things like *I'm lazy, I procrastinate, I can't, it's too hard*. Start keeping track of when you're saying or thinking these things.

Take it a step further and be conscious of what's going on in your life at that moment that's causing you to say it. Be conscious of how quickly it's in your head or comes out of your mouth. Be conscious of the word(s) you're using to describe this. You may find that you're doing it too often. You may even find a relationship between your environment, what's happening at that moment, and how you are describing yourself. Woven together, this becomes your story; it is what you say to explain why things are as they are.

Assignment:

Write the stories you use to explain, justify, or understand the clutter.

I may need this in the future.
I don't have time to organize things.

This is a good exercise to help you focus on what it is that you are doing to yourself. It's NOT meant as a means to beat yourself up. Millions of people do this. We are culturally conditioned to denigrate ourselves. The three thousand ads that we're exposed to each day are not meant to uplift and elevate the spirit. They tell you that it will only happen if you buy a certain product. Just go shopping, buy that next face cream, and on and on and on. We're culturally inscribed to not feel good about ourselves. If we want to feel good, we have to do it to and for ourselves because the messages we see and hear every day are what's moving the negativity forward.

Look around your spaces. What's under the bed, or on the bed, or around the bed, or in the living room? How do your closets look? Start thinking about these spaces, the external baggage. The negative thinking is the *internal* stuff. The baggage is the *external*, the physical manifestation. Sometimes the external manifests as poor health. Sometimes it's the clutter in our lives.

Excess baggage means having more than you actually need. I decided to look up *need* in the dictionary. It means *to have*, to be necessary, to want. Psychologist Eric Erickson describes basic needs as food, water, shelter, clothing. Some modern lists describe similar basic needs and include particular belongings. We are generally pretty good at meeting the basic needs, but I don't think many of us meet our emotional needs very well. And because we are not meeting our emotional needs, we fill our lives with the physical manifestation of that which we really may *not* need. We keep bringing more and more into our homes, into our lives, into our offices. Pretty soon we're surrounded by external baggage of what's really going on in our mind. We're tired and overwhelmed and can't move forward. We come home after spending a day saying unkind things about who we are, and then we look around and simply can't deal with the situation. One reason why you can't deal with this may be because your head is filled with so many negative things!

Beyond our basic needs are our wants and desires. Our *wants* are more purses or shoes or clothes, makeup, anti-aging products, that kind of stuff. Our *desires* may be a better job, maybe world peace, things that are a bit more theoretical, esoteric, and not necessarily physical. I believe we're not able to enjoy our wants and desires because of our clutter. We simply can't move forward.

WHAT IS CLUTTER?

Do you know the comic strip *Peanuts*? One of the characters, Pig Pen, walks around with dirt fluttering and swirling all around himself. I think that's such a great metaphor for what's in our head. It looks like our clutter is surrounding us as we're walking through.

I'm going to suggest that you look at your clutter as the enemy. Clutter is usually a benign term to describe the impact of all the stuff in your life. Clutter can be a few pieces of paper on a table. My table is cluttered. But when you're getting into stacks and piles and messes, and taking a deep breath every time you look at it, that's the enemy. It's not serving your higher good or higher purpose in any way, shape or form.

Clutter occurs for one of two reasons: It's either a chronic condition (discussed in greater detail later in this book) where it feels like we've never really been able to get it together to be organized, or it's situational and often an indication that something is happening in our life. We had a transition where we start accumulating or acquiring things and, as a result, we just start loading up, and then not be able to get back in our game. It becomes too overwhelming. I walk into the homes and offices of many clients and see piles of papers and stuff everywhere. This work that I do is not rocket science, but I encounter people on a regular basis who don't know where to start. It's *that* overwhelming. They can't see a single corner in their space that they can de-clutter quickly. Most of your clutter is a direct result of delaying the decision about what to do with it. We put it down, we put it off, and we don't pick it up again until months, sometimes years later.

Here's what I've observed: people have one hand way out into the future, holding on to that which they think they may need someday. The other hand is holding on to the past, to the items and artifacts that gave meaning to life at the time they came into one's life. Holding on to that which we may need, and that which has already happened, doesn't leave a whole lot of room (literally!) for a level of comfort in the present. It's as if past and future upstage any hope of having an uncluttered present.

Look around your space. What was happening with you when you acquired certain things that you know are no longer serving you? Serving means useful. Is it still useful? Are you using it? Is someone in your home using it? Is it functional? Is it beautiful and lovely? Is it serving your spirit, your intellect, your physical body? Are you looking at an object and thinking *I haven't used that in years*. What was happening when it entered your life? I hear most people say that they have a difficult time letting the clutter go, but when they do, they're not going to replace it. I think that's an important insight because if you think you're going to replace it, it means that you're still going to use that item in a different form.

Do you have control of, or a handle on your clutter? Do you want to just deal with it and not allow it to be a nemesis for you? An assignment I want you to think about is to identify the things in your life that aren't serving you. Do some writing about what it means to have something that *is* serving your life. Aside from food, clothing and shelter and those things that are our basic needs, look at photo frames, greeting cards, piles of paper, miles of files, clothing. Do you have clothing in your closet that you haven't worn for six months or more, doesn't fit, or that just never looked or felt quite right? Those clothes become discouraging to look at, and we feel awful because we don't fit into them anymore. Then we are angry because we stopped (or never started) working out, and since we don't go to the gym, we have a terrible relationship with our body and we feel unlovable. *Sigh....*

Assignment:

What does it mean to you to have something that serves you?

_____
_____
_____
_____
_____
_____
_____
_____
_____
_____
_____
_____
_____

It's part of the double-damning thing we do to ourselves. Our clothes don't serve us and we blew a ton of money on them so that there becomes a financial component to it. Why do we keep clothes that don't fit us? Why do we hold on to them? No wonder we can't move forward! No wonder we don't feel good about ourselves! Clothing, after all, tends to help define success, to define what it means to feel good about my body, and what it means to feel what is the healthy body for Regina. I came out of the womb a size 10. I'll never be smaller than a 10. That's just the way it is for me. And nor would I want to be smaller than a 10 because with my frame and my bone structure, I don't look good smaller than a 10. But it doesn't even matter because it's how I feel about myself.

I had to define what a successful body is for me, but what is a successful mind? What is a successful business? We don't live in a culture that encourages people to create their own definitions. If we did, we wouldn't be buying all that stuff to make us feel better. So I'm suggesting to you that you create your own personal definitions of healthy, of what's good, of what's attractive for you. We do not have to buy into the cultural considerations! This is not a simple task. If it were simple, we would have already done it!

When you decide that you want to change one thing about your life, perhaps redefining success or redefining a healthy body, you're going to want to remind yourself over and over what that is for you. Soon it'll become part of your mantra. Pretty soon, as we move forward, you'll become much stronger of mind. And how we think is the only thing over which we have control. Consider all the ways you believe or want to control a situation or an outcome, or how somebody's going to respond to you or control your income.

There were three months in 2011 where my business really slowed down and I understood that the rubber was about to hit the road. I knew that the clutter in LA had not dried up. I had to completely embrace my own personal mantra of *conceive, believe, achieve.* I had not one moment of doubt. I certainly didn't want to go out and find a job. I believe in myself more that anybody else on the planet! So what I did in those three months of slow-down was to create new workshops. I created a tele-seminar, from which this book was born. I networked and I marketed and every time I saw an e-mail showing a speaker, I wrote to the organization asking if I could speak too. I just didn't stop. I know I have good ideas. I know how to market. And I knew that no matter what, I had to continue believing in my ability to have a successful month because I didn't want to borrow money from Dad. Sometimes that was the only incentive I needed. *I'm not going to borrow money from Dad.* And so far, I haven't. *That's* my measure.

I truly believe that you're going to understand, really know, that you can change your thinking about how you are thinking about your life. Let it be enough that I believe that about you until you start believing it about yourself.

Review and add to your head trash list then make a mark next to whatever is going on around you. Begin to identify what you believe is the excess external baggage in your life. You don't have to do anything about it, just begin to identify it. Later we'll look at what our words and our things say about ourselves. We're going to learn how to separate ourselves from our *things*. Then we will start to physically clear the path on the ground and clear the path in our psyche. My goal is to give you tools that you can use and never have to feel bad or negative about yourself again. The goal is for you to be able to say *I trust myself. I trust that I can move forward and believe it.* Remember that idea about the kid who whistles in the dark because she doesn't want to feel alone or to avoid other things going on? We can whistle in the dark for a little while as this new thing is coming into our consciousness, but even that will disappear when you have trust and faith in yourself.

Notes to myself:

_____
_____
_____
_____
_____
_____
_____
_____
_____
_____
_____
_____
_____
_____
_____
_____
_____
_____

DE-CLUTTER AND DISCOVER

I have worked with many clients who un-cluttered and discovered, and eventually discarded many items in their home and work space that were no longer serving their higher good. It made me think about the type of stuff that we surround ourselves with in order to make ourselves feel a certain way, or to make us respond to life in a particular manner. The clutter and chaos of psychic debris often reflects the clutter and chaos of our living spaces, and somehow we make it okay to look in crowded closets, or at piles of paper and rooms packed with stuff we no longer use or want or desire. Let's see how they match the list of words and phrases that we added to our head trash list.

Do it later is limiting you. *Do it later* is keeping you packed too tightly. *Do it later* is not allowing you to move forward because you're finding that there's no appropriate time to *do it later*. When we put off a task, we find that this task is usually undesirable for some reason. And eventually, the *do it later* attitude allows things to just continue to pile and pile so that getting to it is a daunting task.

What you're experiencing feels unmanageable. And it's holding you back. If you do any kind of journaling, see if you can flesh that out. Is this something that you have always experienced? Much of how we operate in our life is a direct link to our childhood. That is a concept that I resisted for a very long time. I'm an adult. I'm educated. How could my viewpoints and how I walk through life be linked to my childhood? I'm so different from my mother. I'm not at all like my father. Yet there were messages all along about the way that I internalized without even realizing it. I never felt like an accomplished person, that I could be accomplished even though my mother told my sisters and me that we were smart and beautiful.

My mother's internal message to herself, ironically, was completely the opposite, and that's what I was holding on-to. I took on the messages of *I'm not good enough, I'm not smart enough* because that's how she felt about herself. And it wasn't until much later in life that I recognized that these messages were ingrained in me. They were keeping me thinking about myself in negative ways and in ways that were simply not serving me at all.

So the *do it later* attitude is tied into the fact that you're tired and your job is emotionally exhausting. If being tired is keeping you from doing it now, go back. Flash back. What is it about your day that would make you less tired emotionally? Is it finding time to meditate? Look to see where these messages are coming from so you can allow yourself to start freeing up your head-space to create a new way of moving forward. Pay attention to the head-trash messages. You're very fortunate if you have just the *do it later* and *I'm tired*. As you pay more attention to how you're walking through your life, you may come up with a couple more. By *doing it later*, there is resistance. The *doing it later* reflects something bigger.

Assignment:

What are your *do it later* areas?

Our words and our things, what do they say about us? Or rather, what do *we think* they say about us? What do the things we surround ourselves with or hold on to say about us? What do they represent to you? If clothing, what do they say about the fact that they are hanging in your closet?

I get a sense that many folks believe that however they're walking through their lives, they tend to hold on to things that no longer reflect who they are. Holding on may be a reflection of a different time in our life when we romanticize the past, or when we were at our ideal weight. We look back at the past with a great deal of fondness, and with that fondness comes holding on to the baggage of that time without taking into consideration that *this* time of our life has the potential to be, or already is, pretty darned good. I have gone through two big transitional periods in my life. One was when I was acknowledging my lesbian identity, and the other was when I knew I had to leave a long-term relationship. In both instances before I made the actual moves, I found myself reflecting on my next life. I wasn't even looking back in the past. I was looking ahead to what was possible, to what the future might hold.

I also realized that we often hang on to remembrances from the past in the form of stuff. That stuff is not only outdated, it reflects outdated thoughts about who we are. It's all head trash. Negative head trash manifests in the physical. We find ourselves surrounded by artifacts and items that reflect how we feel about ourselves. What we keep adding to our life will continue to remain in our life. If we continue to add items that don't uplift or elevate our spirits, or we don't remove the items that aren't serving us, they will just continue to be in our life without even recognizing that that's what we're doing.

When anything enters our spaces, we immediately assign a "value" to it. Everything has value: milk, paper towels, beautiful art, books. But when the milk carton is empty, the carton no longer has value so we toss the empty into the recycle bin. The milk is gone and we move on. It is a strange irony that we don't think of our stuff in similar ways. If a relationship has broken up, or our taste in decor has changed, why do we insist on holding on to something when it loses its original value? The relationship is gone so move on and let that stuffed bear go!

Where does our stuff come from? Look at the 17 formal dresses in your closet and remember why you have them, where they came from, and maybe the store at which they were purchased. Everybody has stuff. We have a variety of things we love or need. Some of our stuff was acquired on our own, and that's often the favorite bed sheets, books we like to read, and so forth. We bring items into our life for a variety of reasons.

Some of our stuff was given to us by people who are no longer in our lives, perhaps people to whom we don't even speak anymore. I work with many clients who hold on to love letters from boyfriends or girlfriends from a very long time ago. When they look at those letters, they remember that they were loved or that they were young and carefree. Though we haven't seen that person for a long time, letting go of the letters feels like we're abandoning a part of our self who no longer is. I think that's much of the reason why people hold on to things that are given to them by people who are no longer part of their lives. Many us will acquire things from people who gave us stuff with good intentions but we don't need. It doesn't serve us. And yet we display it because the giver may visit some day! I've noticed that people will hold on to something they don't like, want, need, or desire, even if it contributes to their clutter! They give the item value because the person who gifted it to them gave it value.

I know of people who pull out the knick-knacks they don't like when the giver is coming to visit. It becomes very disingenuous where not only are we not serving ourselves, but we're not serving the person who gave it to us. If someone is repeatedly giving you useless gifts, you may find the courage to have a conversation about the giving.

Assignment:

What items have you kept only because someone special gave them to you...but you really don't like them.

_____
_____
_____
_____
_____
_____
_____
_____
_____
_____
_____

Keep a box in your house for the gifts that are not serving you or that are inappropriate. Every couple of months take the box to Goodwill, or re-gift items to someone else. Many families have a tremendous amount of clutter, so a mother may give her daughter the ugly French bowl because the mother doesn't want to make the decision about what to do with it. So family members end up overburdening one another with the things that nobody in the family wants, uses, or desires.

There are many items in people's homes that are mysteries. People don't know where they came from, not because they're not paying attention but because they had them for many years and hadn't used them in a long while. Now they can't remember why they have it or who gave it to them, and they hold on to it because *I may need it someday.* Start reflecting on what is it that you have around you. Where did it come from? What manner is or is it not serving you? How long has it been in your life? How long has it not served you?

When did your stuff become clutter? Because in and of itself, our stuff is just stuff. Individually, they are things, items. But collectively, at some point, for many people, our stuff becomes clutter. I will argue that it becomes clutter when we can no longer find its home. Every item that we need and that we're planning to keep must have a home. So things lying around us are, well, homeless. We've got homes filled with homeless items that become clutter when they no longer serve you and have no home.

Some people will hold on to broken things or picture frames that may be missing a glass. *I'm going to have a glass made one day.* Or they have many beads because one day they're going to make necklaces. People hold on to things that don't have any particular value right now but may have a perceived future value. But today, in the moment, these items just aren't serving us, and no amount of looking at it or moving it from one side of the room to another is going to allow it to serve us unless we take decisive action and fix it or let it go. So if there's no home for your stuff, it becomes clutter. If it's not serving you, it's clutter. If it's broken or useless, it's clutter. Our houses are filled with clutter.

For some people, clutter eventually becomes the enemy because of how it makes us feel when we walk into a room and have to look at it. It becomes the enemy and we feel bad. Nobody or nothing can make us feel a particular way. Our mind is where the control is. But when we encounter certain situations or people, and we feel bad about them, or ugly or fat or stupid or lazy or whatever, the head trash piles on. That's when we encounter the enemy.

The bedroom, for me, is a sanctuary. That's where rejuvenation and rest happens. Yet I've seen bedrooms where half the bed is covered with papers and books and files and pens and notepads and things that are not conducive to rest, meditation, or relaxation. If it's not conducive to the calm, then it's the enemy. Looking at clutter in terms of how it's keeping us blocked, let's think of it as an evil force. I don't know if that's the right term to use, but clutter really is a very negative force. It's the enemy that we have to fight with everything we've got to keep it at bay. It's become the enemy when we can't invite people into our homes or when we find that we have to do a lot of work to move it aside so people can visit and enjoy our space for a little while. If the clutter is making us work double- and triple-time just to be comfortable for a little while, then it's the enemy.

I don't know if this resonates with your *do it later* mantra, but if you were to look around your space, where you live, and where you sleep, and you were to take your short list of head trash and the *do it later*, do you see anything around you that reflects the *do it later*, that are not necessarily your piles but items within the piles?

Many people have weight issues. How they feel about their bodies is as good as what they want. It doesn't matter what the scale says. If you feel healthy and strong, and if you feel that your weight is allowing you to have a healthy, productive life, then what the scale says is irrelevant. But I also believe that people who discard the clothing that no longer fits them may feel like they're giving in to a particular reality about themselves that feels negative. The good news is that we can continue to serve our higher needs even though we don't have evidence of what we think we need right now. Does that make sense?

HAVING STUFF AND KEEPING STUFF

If overflowing bookcases are creating a tripping hazard, your health and safety are compromised. Books can be our friends, and clothes can make us feel and look good and keep us warm, but if these things are causing hazards in our life, then they're the enemy. They're not serving us well.

Some people feel that they just don't have enough. They don't have enough money, yet they end up with dozens of purses, which is very telling because purses hold money. And if they feel that they don't have much money, they'll over-extend credit cards by getting these lovely bags that still have price tags on them. They're trying to fill a hole or to sew things up. They don't feel that they're good enough so they surround themselves with magazines that show them how to be good enough, how to be better, stronger, leaner, meaner, prettier, have better sex, whatever it is, we surround ourselves with magazines when we feel that we're lacking in ability or intelligence in some way. Or we surround ourselves with books when we feel like we don't have enough knowledge for something. I think we often surround ourselves with a lot of stuff because we consciously or unconsciously believe that we are lacking in some area of our life. We continue to shop because at some level we believe our purchases will somehow make our lives better. To that end, I now give "anti-shopping cards" to clients who shop more than the average person. Placed in the wallet in front of the credit card, clients are encouraged to read before they buy:

- Do I need it?
- Will it serve my heart or mind?
- Will it bring me joy?
- Does it cost too much?
- Where will it live in my home?

If you want the anti-shopping card for your wallet, drop me an email: Regina@AClearPath.net.

We purchase things we don't necessarily want and then hold on to them based on cost or some future assumed value. We have one hand stretched way out ahead of us, holding on to that which we may need someday. The other hand reaches far behind us, holding on to what has already happened.

The hand in front is holding on to an unknown, unnamed future we call "someday." We are afraid that something will happen (or not!) if we don't have a particular item for "someday" because, when and if that day finally arrives, and we don't have that thing, we will be unprepared and that is bad. One problem with holding on to "someday" is that most people tend to have a lot of *somedays* on the horizon. Holding on to a lot of *somedays* likely means that you have a lot of stuff everywhere and you won't be able to find what you know you have, if someday ever does arrive!

The hand that we have behind us? The one that holds on to the past? We have a belief that these remnants and artifacts from the past have a particular importance, so important that we have to save them for... what? Are you clear about your stronghold on the past? What is it about these trinkets and letters, old newspapers with the Apollo landing above the fold, clothes from when we were five years old that compel us to save?

I'm grateful every day that my parents are alive. Each year they send a birthday card which I display with the others that I've received. After two weeks, all cards are taken from the shelf and re-read one last time. I save a couple with warmly written sentiments, and I always save the ones from my parents. Each year I replace their cards from the year before. I figured that while I can never know if this birthday is their last birthday with me, I am clear that I need only one card signed by my mother that says, "I love you so much."

A hand in front of us holding on to an unnamed future, and one behind, hanging on to a distant past, is usually responsible for the very clutter we're trying to deal with in the present.

At this juncture I encourage you to cross-reference your list of head trash with the stuff in your space. See where *someday or later* is keeping things piled up. Look at all things. Is there a pattern to what you're holding on to? What are the tasks you put off for later and why? There are certain things in those piles that reflect…what? There's got to be a pattern there. I would be curious to know if you see that there's a pattern in the areas that you feel are very cluttered with a tight hold in either the past, the present, or both.

Assignment:

What are in these piles and what are their similarities?
Think about it broadly.

_____

_____

_____

_____

_____

_____

_____

_____

_____

_____

_____

_____

_____

_____

_____

_____

_____

_____

_____

_____

_____

_____

_____

_____

_____

I would wager that there are similarities and patterns in all of these piles. It may be the idea of junk – junk mail, junky things that you don't need in your life but you're just not ready to send them out of your life. There's got to be something that is reflecting a bigger picture. So look to see what your list of head trash is and how it reflects what you're surrounding yourself with. It's like the formal wear I mentioned earlier; a reflection of what was at that time. What do the things that we're holding on to say about the times that we were living when they came into our lives. I think it's very different for every individual.

The good news is *we're not our stuff*. Stuff is just a temporary reflection of where we're at right now. I appreciate that we're all very powerful people on the inside, that we can create a mindset that changes patterns and changes the relationship we have with our stuff. And once we change our thinking, the next thing that may happen is life will change. So we have this idea that what's happening right now is temporary even though it may have been a part of our life, for a very long time.

At this point in the lifecycle, we know it's temporary because as we change our thinking and change our life, how our stuff is reflecting our life is also going to change. That idea gives me a lot of hope in terms of understanding that change can happen. It happens once we change our thinking about our stuff, and change our thinking about how we're moving through this moment in time. Something's happened to attract you to the concept of the relationship between the stuff in your head and what's under your bed. It may not have been an attraction a month ago or a year ago. There's a shift in your personal universe that is allowing this to transpire in your life. I encourage you to embrace that. The change we want to see may not happen overnight but it's definitely going to happen.

Keep working on changing how you think and talk about your present circumstances. I encourage you to really pay attention to every word that's coming out of your mouth. You want to keep working on it. It's going to be a very dedicated mindset. You've got to trust the process and be patient with the process. But really start choosing thoughts and words that are going to make you feel good about your surroundings, and about where you are in your life. It's completely up to you to make these choices first in your head and then to reflect how the shift is happening from your head to what's happening under your bed. (I just say that because I love the way it rhymes!) Know that you're safe in these changes. You can handle change easily.

Begin to look around you and identify the things you no longer need, want, or desire. What is your next step now that you know that much of your stuff is a reflection of what's going on in your head?

Assignment:

As you change from the concept of head trash to a more positive outlook, begin to identify what you don't need. Which of your items is no longer serving you? And as you go through your week, become very clear about what it is that you don't need. You don't have to do anything about it. Just start looking at it in terms of need, want, and desire.

Sometimes, when I'm in between sessions with a client, I'll ask her or him to put little post-it notes on the items that are no longer needed. When I return, we either discard the items on the spot or have a conversation about what the challenge is about letting them go. But once the post-it note goes onto an item, a decision is being made about it. *I don't need this.* Now the next step is how to eliminate it from one's life.

PUTTING "IT" BACK IN YOUR LIFE

I've seen this over and over again. I've worked with clients who talk about not having enough money or they don't know where it goes. It comes in, it goes out. Financial stuff becomes such a huge issue and yet there will be dozens of handbags. The handbags are not only a manifestation of the physical clutter, but also in some way relates to the idea of stealing financial insecurity. Where do we put our money? Many women put their money in their handbags.

I have observed that there are three components that are ubiquitous parts of the life of any human being: money, stuff, and relationships. And the irony is that most of us are not taught – whether in school or at home - how to deal well and successfully with all or any of these, and it's no wonder that most people have challenges in one or all of these areas. High divorce rates and the proliferation of public storage spaces, speak volumes about how inadequate we are to deal with our stuff.

I'm working on a theory to understand more about how the negative messages run to our head, the head trash. Is there a relationship between what you see in our physical spaces and what you would describe as clutter? Look at your list of head trash and negative thoughts that you tell yourself. What do they say about why you're not doing in your life what you want to be doing, and why the clutter is still a part of your life? Can you see the evidence of the head trash in your clutter?

When you have the sensation of panic because you can't find anything due to the clutter, it's like the feeling of being out of control. Often there will be a consequence. For example, late charges on your credit cards, or papers that don't get filed in time and you lose medical coverage, or your car insurance lapses. There are some serious consequences when your paper work is out of control. When that feeling occurs, how do you handle it? What happens to the head trash? Are you able to keep perspective? Or did your head take off with unkind messages about yourself?

Assignment:

What are you feeling/thinking right now about this?

_____

_____

_____

_____

_____

_____

_____

_____

_____

_____

_____

_____

_____

_____

_____

_____

A matrix was developed a few years ago by Stephen Covey to help people structure their days so that they meet all their goals. A lot of people call that time-management even though they can't manage time at all. The matrix includes: *urgent and important, urgent-not important, not urgent-not important, important but not urgent.* It helps people to prioritize what they want and need to do.

	Urgent	Not Urgent
Important	Broken heater, boiler, power outage, etc.) Calling 911 for emergencies Child fell, skinned her knee! 1	Meditation time/ "unwind" time Catching up with friends and family members Mental and physical health 2
Not Important	3 Distractions/interruptions from co-workers who try to make their "urgent" your "urgent"	4 Catching up with recorded TV shows Going to a movie Catching up with Facebook

Many of the *urgent not important* issues tend to get us sidetracked during our day. Others decide that their issue is very important and that we need to pay attention to it. This happens often with people who work in a big office or have a family that they're taking care of. Children believe that whatever they have say to you is the most important thing for both of you right in that moment. I was talking with a client the other day who works from home. The neighbors think it's okay to knock on her door constantly. Suddenly their urgent becomes your urgent when it's not even an issue that's very important to you.

The matrix helps us set boundaries and prioritize the tasks of the day. For example, open the mail as it comes in everyday rather than let it pile up. Once you develop that habit, the pile will shrink. The meaning behind the pile will also shrink as things feel much more doable.

IDENTIFYING WHAT YOU NEED

How do you get a handle on what you need and don't need in your life? Review the notes you made in earlier chapters. What does not serve you? Remember the negative messages? They don't serve us at all. So let's explore our investment in maintaining a status quo of negative thoughts about ourselves rather than move forward as we'd like.

Why do we hold on to negative things, thoughts, or positions that don't serve us? What might happen if most of your thoughts were positive and uplifting? Does that sound like something that you could do or does it sound impossible, maybe not even realistic? What's the investment in maintaining the negativity and what's the fear of changing the thinking? What's the story behind the negative thinking? We're not used to exploring the *why* of our thinking, for example, or the *why* about how we *think* we look. I had to really drill down and find out why it is that I insist on tearing myself up and putting myself down.

People would say to me, "You look great today." My response was always, "Oh no, no I don't." Why did I say that??? Did I want elicit more compliments? Did I truly believe I did not look good? And if I really believed that then, do I still believe it now? By negating the compliment, am I then calling that person a liar? The idea of negative talk moving around in our head comes from somewhere. What are the reasons for still holding on to the psychic debris?

Assignment:

Why do you think you hold on to the things in your brain that don't serve you?

_____

_____

_____

_____

_____

_____

_____

_____

_____

_____

_____

_____

_____

_____

_____

_____

_____

_____

_____

_____

_____

_____

_____

_____

_____

_____

_____

Many people, I believe, are not in tune with the *whys* of what they think and what they do. Our tendency is to do things out of habit. How many times have we been in our workplace when someone says "Ugh! It's Monday." Monday is a day to start anew, but the consensus is that there is a long week ahead and the mood becomes depressed. It's cloudy, the weather is lousy, and you buy in to the mood, the tone, the feeling. It's like auto-response. Suddenly your Monday is a drag. You may have started the day feeling good and spry and ready to go but the negative atmosphere brings you right down. We have a tendency to not really pay as much attention to what's entering our brain or coming out of our mouth, especially as we attempt the group-think status quo of a workplace. Perhaps if we paid more attention to the incoming and outgoing messages, we would start hearing more positive language and begin to make some changes.

Assignment:

Begin taking notes on your auto-response to such things as day of the week (TGIF!), or rain in the forecast, or someone's good fortune (they're luckier than me), a friend's cold (I always get what's going around). How do suppose this "group think" contributes to your overall imagine of your own life?

_____
_____
_____
_____
_____

INVESTING IN THINGS WE DO NOT SEE

We put tremendous pressure on ourselves to be as close to perfect as possible. I don't know if we do that consciously, but *unconsciously* we don't like looking stupid or making a mistake, or wasting money. So we maintain evidence of what we think are our inadequacies. And we don't have to be the only owner. There's a great commercial on TV right now that depicts a man polishing and detailing his car. A woman stands next to him and says, "I don't know if you want to do that right now." He asks, "Who are you." She responds, "I'm the second owner." He says, "I just bought this car brand new." She says, "I understand that but I'm going to buy it right after you."

I love this! It's so linear. There's a seamlessness about ownership, about possession, about a second life. We just don't see in our daily lives, maybe not at all! When we invest in things, are we investing in the status quo? What is this stuff to us? How did it become so important that we find ourselves in clutter without the ability to move freely through our spaces? We simply maintain the clutter. When I mention that, what do you feel?

Assignment:

Reflect on the above paragraph. What does that bring up for you?

_____

_____

We usually hold on to things because we equate the letting go of an item with letting go of the person who gifted us with it. The item becomes the personification of the person. There are people with hoarding disorders who believe they cannot part with stuff because each object has a life on some level. These are not stupid people. Many with this disorder are very smart people who are well-educated and have high IQ. They reasonably know that the yogurt container isn't a living, breathing thing, but the brain creates a scenario that personifies the object. Therefore one might think *I better take the lid off the container before I put it in the trash bin because it's going to get humid on the inside and it won't like that.*

We give items some type of life, perhaps associated with the giver of the item, which then makes us feel guilty or sad about letting it go. I've learned to rely on my heart for the good memories; I don't necessarily need an item to prove I was on a fabulous vacation. We also hold on to things that are serving us negatively: we may not like the person anymore. For example, the item was from a former lover, or the clothing doesn't fit us any longer, but we hold on to the item or clothing which in turn allows us to wallow in the bad feelings most of the time. So the items that aren't serving us, whether because we don't like them or they remind us of somebody, take on a life of their own because of how we have attached meaning to them.

We may not know exactly the origins of why we have our peculiarities, but it's interesting to think back and ask, "What was my first pen? How did I feel when I held it in my hand? Did it make my writing look better? Did I look smarter with it?" Maybe you just really liked that style of pen, but there was something going on that triggered a strong relationship to that particular writing instrument. So now you have almost a thousand of them! You write with only one hand, even though you have two, yet you now have a thousand pens! Same thing with shoes. Some folks have dozens or hundreds of pairs of shoes, yet we have only two feet and can wear only one pair at a time. It's just breaking things down to the least common denominator, which helps you through the thought process. You can do the Socratic method with yourself.

But why do it, especially when it comes to making some of the harder decisions? Ask yourself, *why is it so hard for me to get rid of this? What did it mean to me at the time I acquired it? How did I feel with it? How do I feel about it now?* Letting go is no easy task, as evidenced by how we have filled our spaces. If it were easy, you wouldn't be reading this book and I'd be pushing papers somewhere at some office. But we're physical, emotional, causatively and behaviorally human, so we respond to our stuff in such broad ranges of ways. Become more conscious about your physical environment and start to do the clearing. Pay attention to the things that are easy for you to move away from your life, and pay attention to the things about which you're waffling, and why. Pay attention to long-held items. Why do they remain a part of your life?

I have noticed that people tend to keep hold of the past and a firm grasp on the future. They have one hand behind them holding on to that which once was, that which has already happened, a past that has already passed. Holding on to all the memories ... it's as though people don't trust that they'll continue to experience good times, or they lack faith they'll remember a good deed without the very item they're holding in their hand.

We seem to have a firm grasp on that which they may need someday. Someday is one day, or no day, or forever away. Someday is rarely identified in terms of who, what, when, where, or why. It is an unknown future, an event that may or may not happen but we hold on to these artifacts for future use because... YOU NEVER KNOW when you may need it!

And herein lies the one of the bigger challenges associated with working toward clearing the path. Several times in this book I describe our relationships to our stuff in terms of our beliefs about the past and the future. This is a message worth repeating. I have seen a lot of significant decluttering come on the heels of taking the message to heart. We have one hand in the past holding on to that which has already happened, and one hand in the future, holding on to that which may never happen. Essentially we are allowing the past and future trump our ability to be comfortable in the present. It cannot be overstated that we live as if the future and past are more important to how we want to live today.

Assignment:

Select an item or two and ponder why you hold on to them if they're not serving you now.

_____

_____

Here's something else to think about: What does it mean to have *enough*? To be enough? To feel worthy enough? In terms of the items around your space can you come up with a number to answer questions about how many shoes, pens, bags, books, and black slacks... are enough?

Assignment:

Identify the "enough factor" for two or three categories of items. Count the number of items in each category you currently own and see if you can whittle down the category according to an exact number.

Identify other items in your space that you've had a hard time letting go, even though you know you'll never use again. Decide what you're willing to give up, and with a pad of small post-its, tag those items you no longer need, want, desire, or which have outlived its value. You don't have to let things go right away. Just tag them and start moving them away from your life slowly.

The process of letting go and the process of physically removing the things that no longer serve you is not going to happen overnight. As you move through these new actions, you'll likely feel vulnerable and on shaky ground. Sit with those feelings to try to understand. You're holding on to things or people who are no longer in your life for whatever reason. Letting go of things may bring up some issues about yourself and about others in your life. It might be a good idea to have a mental health provider on hand because the challenge of letting go is not an easy process for us. It will tend to bring up memories and feelings ranging from inadequacy to shoulda-woulda-coulda, missed opportunity, and a wide array of past issues. Psychiatrist Melva Green, coauthor of *Breathing Room: Open Your Heart by Decluttering your Home* writes, "Just because something made you happy in the past doesn't mean you have to keep it forever."

I've seen this happen with people who are going through a de-cluttering process. There's a real freedom in finding new space, but there may also be real sadness. I'm going to share a real-life experience I had with my mother.

My mother has a hard time letting go of things. She doesn't have a hoarding disorder as such but she's chronically disorganized. She also identifies her wonderfulness through her things. While she's led an incredibly interesting life, she doesn't take credit for much. She has a lot of "I wish" statements: "I wish one of my kids….", "I wish I had paid more…", "I wish I had done that…". She feels inadequate, and even though her daughters tell her, "Look at us. We're all pretty cool women!" She feels like she missed out.

Three years ago I de-cluttered her of a lot of books; my job was to put the books in boxes. I watched her gently hold and open the book, move her fingers lovingly through the index; every page had context and meaning. There were books of art and music and languages. As I was learning more about her love of literature, music, and color, she disparaged herself because she never did learn Russian, that she never painted the great masterpiece, or wrote the perfect song. It brought up so many feelings of inadequacy, but she was downsizing her space and knew she had to let them go.

I checked in with her about her anxiety level as we were going through this process. On a scale of 1 to 100, her anxiety level on the first day was about 90. The next day it was 60, and two weeks later it was pretty much zero. She was able to acknowledge that at age 75, whatever she paints is pretty darned good. But the process and willingness of letting go produced some hard feelings for her. I want you to be aware of the possibility of that in your life.

THE CLEAR PATH WAY

One of the ways that you're going to be able to maintain a cleared path is to feed your head with positive messages about who you are, what your goals are, and how you want to move forward in your life. One way to do this is what I call the art and practice of positive affirmation. An affirmation is a positive statement or assertion. It's a form of meditation or repetition, and a statement of the existence or truth of something. When I do meditation or affirmation, I speak as though the actual sentiment is already occurring in my life. So when I do affirmations for positive cash flow, for example, I speak this affirmation: *My calendar is filled with appointments with wonderful clients ready for a big change in their lives* - as though the cash flow that I intend for my life is already in my life. It's a belief that the cash flow is actually here.

Metaphysical teaching, which is about spirituality or universality, suggests that everything you need to know is already inside of you. It's now a matter of connecting with it. This is how I practice affirmation, believing that it's already here. I know that there are many books on positive thinking. In 1987 I came across the book *You Can Heal Your Life* by Louise Hay. It first introduced me to this idea of creating a different mindset and has since profoundly influenced my life.

Whenever I do career coaching with a client, I give them the Louise Hay book *You Can Heal Your Life* and Napoleon Hill's *Think and Grow Rich*. Those two books have equally influenced me both professionally and personally.

You Can Heal Your Life. Louise Hay is alive and well and in her early 90s now and still doing presentations. In her career as a psychologist, she was one of the very few people in this country who reached out to early HIV/AIDS patients. When no one else would touch them, Louise Hay embraced them. There was so much fear about dying, and these young men were dying so quickly. Louise helped them get in touch with inner child issues and talked with them about forgiveness. She helped them create a different mindset, and as a result, the book *You Can Heal Your Life* was born. Louise Hay takes the reader on a journey to be able to deal with the wreckage of the past, offering love and confidence and acceptance.

Louise has "The List" in her book. It's an A through Z list which names nearly every type of physical ailment that the body might experience, along with a suggestion of a metaphysical reason why this ailment is in one's life. It is accompanied by a positive affirmation so one may move these ailments out of one's life. Over the years I've come to rely upon this book should something feel funny in my body. I rarely get sick, luckily, so the book has become a reference for others when they share their issues with me. For example, recently a good friend of mine was diagnosed with diabetes. We wondered what was happening in her life, or what may be a metaphysical reason for this occurrence. Hay suggests that diabetes may represent a *longing for what might have been. A great need for control. Deep Sorrow. No sweetness left.*

There are many metaphysical reasons why an illness might come into our lives. This is not an exact science. It's a component to western practices of medicine, I believe. But

74

Louise's book is about changing your life through positive thinking. I probably could have included other books but this is the one that speaks to me. Louise has a daily affirmation calendar that I keep on my countertop next to my coffee pot. The affirmations help me to remember how to stay in the flow and to remain positive. Her internet address is www.LouiseHay.com.

Reading Hill's *Think and Grow Rich* was a game-changer for me. His teaching gave words to what I knew to be true about my life and the power I feel walking the path of gratitude and positive thinking. His credo, "conceive, believe, achieve" is what got me through my doctoral dissertation, although I didn't discover Hill until a decade later. Part of my morning meditation practice includes a reciting of what I call "The Plan," crafted from Hill's suggestions from Chapter Two of that book.

Affirmations replace the head trash. A while back I was helping a client clear his storage locker and, admittedly, there were some parts of that day when I was just miserable. His locker was a disaster, complete with dead rodents, and he didn't want to let go of anything which was making my work very difficult. Rather than give in to what felt like misery, I began talking to myself about how good it felt to have such physical work; I still feel physically strong in my mid-fifties. I didn't allow myself to buy into the bad feelings. I created mantras in my head to affirm and reaffirm that I was helping someone downsize from expensive storage space, that I felt grateful for the work. It helped change the day from misery into delight. It became less about me and more about how I was helping somebody else move forward in his life. The more upbeat I felt, the more my client could see the wisdom in letting go of the stuff that had little meaning and costing a lot to keep. When a negative thought hits my head, I'm so tuned into now changing it around and making it positive and better. Creating a different mindset about my life has completely changed my life.

I ritually do affirmations each morning. I also write and meditate. I get up by 6:00 AM and gather my coffee and notebook. I take that time to put myself in a healthy frame of mind. It's not difficult at all, taking that time in the morning. Then throughout the day, rather than complain about traffic, I'm so grateful that I have a car. It changes things. The negative just does not linger. I forgive past experiences. I'm willing to learn something new every day. I love myself and think joyful, happy thoughts which is the quickest way to create a wonderful life. I look in the mirror each morning and evening and say, "I love you so much!" Who else is going to tell me that with so much verve?! You know what I'm saying? It has to come from deep down. I have to feel it. Self-love is an inside job.

Another affirmation that I choose to believe is that I have unlimited potential. It's staying in a positive flow. My needs will be met. I moved into my apartment three years ago. When I first moved in, there were a couple of months in my business where work was short in coming. I was welcoming more work but it wasn't coming into my life. Still, I knew that I'd always be able to pay my rent. I knew this unequivocally, without question. *I believe in Regina, and my needs are always met.* I say that, over and over again. When I'm feeling anxious, I know my needs are being met. I'm happy, joyous, and free. The way I understand it is this: my needs are always met because I've learned to be flexible about how they can be met.

Assignment:
Write your own affirmations and commit to repeating them daily.

_____
_____
_____
_____
_____
_____
_____
_____
_____
_____
_____
_____
_____
_____
_____
_____
_____
_____
_____
_____
_____
_____
_____
_____

One of the things that I hope you get from this book is that your brain will believe every single thing you tell it. Everything. If you say something to yourself repeatedly, you will believe it and own it and will walk that way. If you repeatedly tell yourself that you can't do something or you don't know something or you're too lazy or fat or whatever it is, you're going to believe it. You can elevate yourself as easily as you put yourself down. If you have a choice, elevate!!

Using affirmations, get into a new habit of uplifting and elevating. You can uplift and elevate yourself and your relationships with the people at work or home or in your community. Start today! At the end of the day, you will feel energized and, perhaps like me, feel that you really made a difference in somebody's life, despite the moments through the day when you thought you couldn't do another thing.

There is a metaphysical reason why things happen in your life and there is an affirmation to help rid yourself of it. Begin the practice of clearing your mind of negative thoughts /psychic debris /head trash, and fill it with positive energy. It needs to become a routine. You might want to put a post-it note somewhere to remember to affirm and reaffirm all the good that is going on in your life. You might want to create an affirmation on the de-clutter process. Something like "I am lovingly removing things from my life, and giving it out to the universe for whoever needs it." This will help you meet your de-clutter goals. Just as you develop the art and practice of creating positive information in your head, there is also an art and practice of clearing your spaces. I always believe that less is more.

Dealing with clutter is a matter of understanding what you don't need and becoming comfortable with the *less is more* mantra. I was at the California Women's Conference where they had give-away gift bags filled with swag. While everyone loves freebies, I can't help but think of the clutter that's already out there! Somebody said, "Well, they give you all these things!" To which I suggested that she doesn't have to take the bag, or take home everything in the bag. I'd rather that the company handing out the bags deal with the burden of hauling the stuff away, rather than place that burden on myself!

I volunteer every year at the Los Angeles Gay and Lesbian OutFest Film Festival, and every year we get a shirt that we have to wear when we're managing the theaters. And every year at the end of OutFest, I donate my shirt to Goodwill. I don't need it in my closet. But this year they asked us to wear last year's shirt. I didn't have it! But guess what? I borrowed one from another volunteer! It worked out! I trust the process of life; all right and good action takes place in my life. I believe this.

So it's really a matter of not taking home what people are giving away, and not purchasing more than you need just because something is on sale. When you're in the de-clutter process and it's changing how you feel about what you want in your space, you begin to see that a sale is no bargain because you end up with more than what you need. You may be saving $3 to $5 but the annoyance and the aggravation you feel with more stuff you're not actually using or consuming really isn't worth it. Less truly *is* more.

When I buy ink for my printer there is a $7 saving when I purchase the economy pack which includes "free" photo paper. I don't print my photos! Staying clutter-free can become a moral dilemma.

Assignment:

Look around your space. Do you have stuff that you bought because it was on sale but that you never use? What are these items? What were you thinking when you purchased them?

_____
_____
_____
_____
_____
_____
_____
_____
_____
_____
_____
_____
_____
_____
_____
_____
_____
_____
_____
_____
_____

Chronic Disorganization:
The key word is "Chronic"

The other day I walked into a home and here's what I saw - nearly every table surface was covered with a combination of these items: unopened mail, keys, empty boxes, newspapers, candles, blank envelopes, blouses (or some type of clothing), candles, drinking glasses/unwashed dishes, Kleenex boxes, books, magazines, hand weights, dog food, and Bed, Bath, and Beyond coupons.

Throughout my tour of the house, my client, a smart, 50-something female, expressed feelings of shame, humiliation, embarrassment, frustration, and, on occasion, humor, as she explained to me the whys and wherefores of the cluttered piles before us:

- I know this area looks horrible, I meant to clean it but the day I started, the plumbing in the kitchen went out and I became distracted.
- This table should be used for crafting with my daughter, but the crafting supplies are behind that big box and we have to go through the box before we can get to the supplies.
- I've never had a system for mail - that's why the piles are everywhere!
- I have duplicates of everything because I can never find what I need when I need it!
- That pile of laundry has been there for so long I don't know what is clean or dirty anymore!

When I first began organizing I walked into many of these homes where stuff was just everywhere. Quite honestly I wasn't really sure why people weren't able to keep their things more orderly, or why, six months after I left their home newly de-cluttered and organized, they'd call again telling me, "it's back!"

In any event I wasn't sure what I was really looking at when I saw miles of piles, and 8-tracks, and cables. Here I stood, in the homes of some really fabulous and amazing people, mostly women, whose houses were an unmitigated disaster, a train wreck if you will, with the majority of clients completely bewildered by how it got that way and why it stays that way.

I have come to learn that what I was looking at was likely what I've come to know as "chronic disorganization." Chronic disorganization (CD) is not a diagnosis per se. Coined in the late 1990s by my friend and colleague, Judith Kolberg, CD is an observed set of behaviors that result in a variety of outcomes. First, a CD person has likely been dealing with disorganization all their life. I describe this as someone born with a brain type that's never allowed them to get their act together. Second, the CD person is in possession of a lot of "how to organize" books. The problem with this, is that books of this type are generally written for someone like me, not for the CD person. Another hallmark of the CD person is that chronic disorganization can impair the quality of one's life - from being chronically late, to unconsciously turning bedrooms into storage rooms.

Chronic disorganization is usually related to how one is hard-wired from birth. In my family of six, four of us have strong tendencies to organize and maintain an organized space, and the other two are chronically disorganized. CD has to with the brain, specifically the part of the brain called the Executive Function.

Think of Executive Function (EF) as the CEO, or dash-board, of our brain. Located in the frontal lobe region, EF makes sure we show up to work when we're supposed to. When the EF is firing on all pistons, we can check off our "to do" lists, and make and meet our goals. If we have to send a birthday card, our EF ensures that we mail it on time. A properly working EF allows us to focus on tasks, manage our emotions, and access our working memories.

When the EF is tweaked, or not working as well as de-signed, things can really pile up! One scenario:

Emily leaves work about 40 minutes later than planned be-cause she decided at the last minute to make one more cli-ent call which went on forever. She had a short errand list for the way home but leaving late put her behind schedule and the dry cleaners would have to wait until tomorrow. A bit frazzled and frustrated Emily, grabs the mail from the box, opens a notice from the library and reads that her "hold" books have been re-shelved because she wasn't able to pick them up in time.

There's nothing to eat in the house because Emily ran out of time to hit the grocery store. She's now frantically look-ing for a take-out menu because she just remembered that she invited her best friend over to watch a few episodes of "Orange is the New Black." Grateful that she managed to pay her cable bill on time, Emily stops short when she real-

izes that she forgot to pay the bill on her landline. Looking through piles for her mobile phone so she can place the call for take out, she feels like she's about to have a heart attack when she discovers her phone is dead. "Crap!" She yells to the air... "Now where the hell is my phone charger?"

Here's what else I've observed about Emily: she's funny, super smart, has dozens of friends and neighbors who adore her. A high-powered executive at a major health care company, earning a mid-range, six-figure income, Emily is creative, loves to draw, paints with watercolors, and has lovely taste in clothes and in art.

Despite and in spite of her awesomeness, Emily is chronically disorganized. She finds it difficult to stay on task and arrive to places on time. She is well-intentioned but has a hard time completing everything on her to-do list. Emily loves her friends but somehow falls short when it comes to remembering to mail cards. She's neither stupid nor lazy. Instead, she seems to have been born with a brain type that has never allowed her to keep her stuff together.

I have a strong interest in chronic disorganization because I think a lot of the people who need the help of a professional organizer are chronically disorganized.

And the "chronic" in chronic disorganization means that the problems inherent to CD will remain unless things change, or shift, the very habits, behaviors, and attitudes that contribute to creating the clutter. One may very well have to change, shift, or tweak their relationship to their environment, and perhaps with the people with whom they live.

Clutter is an accumulation of similar or disparate items that don't seem live anywhere in particular within the confines of your home. One of the reasons why clutter builds in a particular place is probably because you can't figure out where it's supposed to live, or how long it needs to be kept. Added to this pile of stuff, are the habits that continue to create it. One habit could be lousy time-management skills - you make an honest attempt to clear the pile but run out of time to complete the task.

Our habits feel ingrained, as though part of our DNA. But since our habits developed over time by our very own actions, they can change over time in a similar way. Are you able to identify the habits that contribute to your clutter and the ones that keep everything from caving in? Which behaviors or attitudes should stick around and which should go out with the clutter?

We will often engage in a habit without even knowing we are doing this. We do it without thinking. But in order to change or shift how we do things, we need to become aware of what we are doing and why.

Try this exercise: Pretend you are a helicopter pilot. Hover above and around you for a few days. Pay close attention to everything you do from the moment you put your feet on the floor in the morning, to the moment they go back up on the bed at night. What does it mean to be you habit-wise? When, where, how do you brush your teeth and why then and there? Where does your mail go once you get it from the box? How exactly does laundry get done? When, where, how does cleaning get done and why do you choose to clean in the order that you do? How do you prepare/eat food? Shower and dress?

This exercise will require some focus. You may only be able to become aware of your habits in snatches - but for sure look at the good habits you bring, as well as those that you think contribute to the clutter, because those are the very ones that you'll want to shift in order to help you maintain your de-cluttered spaces.

Hyper-vigilance to one's chronic disorganization is key to keeping the clutter at bay. Hiring a professional organizer to help clear the clutter, and working with an organizer coach to help change habits are great maintenance steps. Life transitions such as marriage, childbirth, new job/home, divorce - all these things can easily contribute to tripping up even the most organized person. For the CD, backsliding is not infrequent. Understanding the chronic nature of chronic disorganization is imperative to your emotional, physical, and environmental well-being.

THE PHYSICAL ACT OF DE-CLUTTERING

Open space is uncluttered space. When you are de-cluttering, break the work down into small sections that are manageable for you. Recognize all the places where clutter is gathering in your space and tag it. Prioritize the area you want to clear first. Write it down. Seeing it on paper will help you make it manageable. Some organizers, myself included will sometimes work with a client who is surrounded by so much stuff that the client becomes frustrated working in just one area. I've learned to put a sheet over the other spaces to block their visibility so that the client is able to do the task at hand. Do whatever you can to stay focused whether it's covering other clutter or setting a timer for the amount of time that you've decided you should give it. Try everything. And be sure to put it on your calendar so that you deliberately set aside the time to do the work.

For every hour you spend de-cluttering, you need one hour to reintegrate what you plan to keep. Everything that you're going to keep must have a home. Picture the first area that you want to clear and get it on the calendar. On the day you selected, create a staging area where you will sort your things.

If you're doing the garage, the driveway is a great staging area. If you're doing the closet, the hallway works as a staging area. Sometimes, the room that you're working in is very crowded, so you might use another room for staging. The staging area is divided into sorting sections. So, for example, the area closest to your front door is where you will have the donation pile. Right behind that is where you will put the items you want to recycle. Trash will go near the back door. The items you want to keep should be the smallest pile and will stay near the area where it will live.

Sorting piles are: trash, keep, recycle, and donate. There could be a pile called "not mine, need to give back to the person it belongs to." There could be a pile called "gifts I want to give people." You may have other piles. There may be piles of donations to a variety of places like schools or libraries in addition to Goodwill. But basically the four sorting piles are trash, keep, recycle, and donate.

Remember, for every hour you spend in the act of un-cluttering, you'll want another hour to reintegrate the stuff you plan to keep, and take out of the house the stuff that's not staying. If you're going to do your desk, give yourself a good two to three hours to go through your pile of papers which is an arduous task. Going through a garage is easier, it seems, because the items are bigger and more identifiable. It's easier to make quicker decisions. Going through paper takes a heck of a lot more time than going through a linen closet. As you start the process of de-cluttering, begin to gauge how much time you're spending at each task. If it took you two hours to do a bookcase, and at the end of two hours, you don't feel like you are able to put things back again, then know that the next time you do this you'll need more time. Or, do less in the same amount of time. Ultimately, you don't want a mess after you de-clutter.

De-cluttering is a 3-part process: 1.) decide what you don't need; 2.) take stuff away (recycle/donate/trash); and 3.) put away what you intend to keep.

I de-cluttered a bathroom recently and put an old sheet in the middle of the floor. Everything from every cabinet, every cupboard was dumped out onto the sheet. When I had everything on the sheet, I had a bird's eye view on how many of each item was actually there. In fact, I recently did a hall closet this way. It had many bathroom things including extra rolls of toilet paper, toothbrushes, toothpaste. As we were about to start integrating keeper items back into the closet, I stopped and I said, "Let's look at the bathrooms." There were two bathrooms and I found more items that could have gone with these other piles. So we did the bathrooms simultaneously because they and the closet held similar items. It took two of us about four and a half hours to do the closet and the two bathrooms. We used a combination of purchased containers and small boxes with the lids cut off to corral the "keep" items and the effect of our efforts was gratifying.

I work alongside the people who hire me. With one family, everything we touched came out. Everything. We put it all into the living room. My clients sorted items for trash, items to donate. We had a huge box of unopened hotel shampoos and soaps for a battered women shelter. As I brought items out, they sorted. They were making the decisions about what to keep and what goes. To get an area completely finished in the time you allotted, take everything out of the area. Seriously. Dump drawers over an old sheet or towel so that you catch everything that comes out of the drawer.

Some examples: if you had a drawer filled with hair ribbons, dump the drawer over, sort the different colors or types of ribbons into a baggie. Roll up the baggies and put them in the drawer. When you wear a particular outfit, pick the baggie with the appropriate ribbon color.

Whenever you're taking out and putting back a item often, place it in an area in the drawer for ease of use. I used to go to Palm Desert often and do yard work at my friend's house. I love doing yard work. She had a hose on the front patio of her house. The hose was unwound and out of the container that was supposed to hold it. The container was a big metal bowl which really is very inconvenient. I mean, it's a really stupid hose holder. So I was looking at it while rolling the hose back into the bowl, thinking *this is a perfect example of why we need to be able to put things back easily. If it's not easy, we aren't going to do it.*

My friend pulled out the hose later in the day, and I noticed that she didn't wrap it up when she was finished with it. I asked why. Her response, "Because it's a pain in the ass." Case closed! Make retrieving and returning items easy to do.

If you are making drawers organized and usable, measure your drawer's depth, width, and length. Find dividers that fit in the drawers. Underneath the kitchen sink, for example, is cleanser, furniture polish, cleaning supplies, dishwasher detergent, etc. To contain these items I use a bussers tray - the kind you see at a restaurant for cleaning the table and putting everything into that dirty-dishes tray. I have one underneath my kitchen sink. It pulls out easily because it's plastic, and you'll find similar types of baskets and trays at a home improvement store. Take advantage of the really great inexpensive drawer and beneath-the-sink organizers. And don't forget to measure the space. And don't overfill the containers once you've got them in place!

When you're tackling your closet, the first thing to do is remove all the hangers that don't have anything on them. That frees up a lot of space. Start judiciously looking at your clothing and making those decisions. Give yourself time. If you don't take the time, you won't complete the project. If it's not on the calendar, chances are you might not even start the project.

Project manage your de-clutter goals. Walk through every cluttered area of your place with an iPad or notebook. Make a list of all the areas that you want to tackle. Be specific - what do you want to do with the stuff in that space? What do you want the space to become after it's been cleared? Then, prioritize: easiest to most difficult, vice versa, or whatever makes sense. Next, commit to a year (or more) of de-cluttering by blocking two to four hours a week to work on your projects. Calendar the dates and times. Be specific, be measurable. Involve family and/or close friends. Stay true to you. It's your level of comfort we're talking about here. Decide on the areas where you may need help because of physical or emotional challenges. Ask for help in advance of the project so friends or professionals can mark their calendar too. Give it a year, give it two! Heck, you're going to be two years older anyway, may as well have a nice cleared space to show for it!

Assignment:

It's time to grab the iPad or notebook and pen and start your lists for what needs to be cleared. Then put the list in priority order. Then fill your calendar with dates to de-clutter!

_____
_____
_____
_____
_____
_____
_____
_____
_____
_____
_____
_____
_____
_____
_____
_____
_____
_____
_____
_____
_____
_____
_____
_____
_____
_____

The next two chapters will introduce you to Thomas and Max. They both have clutter issues and are tackling them in different ways.

One Reporter's Opinion

My friend Thomas is a writer and scholar. We met for lunch the other day because I wanted to ask his permission to use his comments for the second edition of this book. In June of this year he began writing to me about his de-clutter process while in the throes of reading the first edition of this book.

Waiting for our meal to arrive, Thomas takes out a pen that I admire:

Regina: Nice pen, Thomas.

Thomas: Would you like to keep it? I'm finding I have a lot of pens. Since I read your book, I am giving things away all the time. Sometimes you want to give it to a good home, you know?

We talked about his impression of *things* since he began his de-cluttering process. He shows a marked degree of insightfulness when he says, "I see that I hold onto to some of the painful memories to show myself how far I've come in my life." Or, "I notice that I assign meaning to things based on how an object has come into my life." The more we talked the more thoughtful he became when he admitted that clutter piles up because, "I simply don't act on it as soon as it enters my space. It just piles up."

And from Thomas's earlier emails when he began the process:

"Material compensation" is an expression that popped into my head when I was contemplating buying a book because I felt badly about something. It is why some of us become packrats. And you get at it in your book. We buy material things to fill the emotional absences in our lives. (Among the books in my piles is one with selected essays of Emerson, including his classic piece, "Compensation." Perhaps that will help me better understand the "compensation" I seek in material things.)

That phrase *material compensation* resonates with me too. I walk into many homes and see the evidence of shopping for stuff not needed. How do I know it's not needed? Because clothing, books, and kitchen gadgets are still bagged and boxed with prices tags on them. And I hear a common lament: "I don't know why I bought this."

Assignment:

This is for someone whose shopping habits don't make you feel good about yourself (or if you think you shop too much). Using Thomas's story as an example, see if you can identify some of the real reasons you shop and buy stuff you don't need.

_____
_____
_____
_____
_____
_____
_____

Another from Thomas:

Today, Regina, I am celebrating a surfeit of shorts. As I began the current process of purging, I threw several pairs of shorts into my giveaway pile, including a favorite pair that had become damaged when bleach spilled on them in the laundry basket. I thought I would have to go to Target to replace them. Determined as I was yesterday to fill a full shopping bag with stuff, I pulled all my shorts out of the closet (as well as my jeans and khakis). I found a couple more pairs to give away. But, I also found a few good pair that I forgot I bought. Well, I'm going to save a few bucks this summer as I won't need to buy another pair of shorts! Indeed, I'll be saving next summer too. Why am I telling you all this? Because I discovered another benefit of de-cluttering. You find hidden treasures, things you have (and may need) but became lost amidst the junk.

I love the ways in which Thomas is a witness to both sides of the value of de-cluttering. He is learning to adjust his thinking about need, want, and desire. He writes later that he did indeed go to Target but only to purchase sundry items like detergent and dental floss. In the process of letting go he had acquired a lot of insight.

One more:

I had decided while reading your book (at the laundry mat) that I had to act on the insights (some of which corresponded my own thoughts about my packrattedness). One of the things in the pile (in the picture I texted you) was an old Indiana Jones field bag that I no longer use because a strap broke. I have since replaced it, but kept the thing for sentimental reasons. It is out of my apartment and gone from my life. I should note though that sometimes we hang onto things not because they remind us of people with whom we had difficult breakups, but often because they remind us of wonderful moments we had. I still have a T-shirt I barely wear because it was the last thing my grandmother Nonny bought me before Alzheimer's took her away from me. And I have a hat that a kind woman gave me on a plane flight, reminded me of her generosity at a difficult time in my life. Maybe I should give that ball cap to you. Do you need a spare baseball cap? Know someone who does?

I gladly accepted Thomas's cap. It has a special place on my bookshelf and will serve, for as long as it's in my life, as a lovely reminder of his process to create new, open spaces in his life, his heart, his home.

Meet Max Wong

Meet Max Wong: blogger, producer, community do-gooder, and a formally cluttered person.

On November 1, 2001, Max took stock of her very cluttered Los Angeles house. Feeling frustrated and demoralized by the extent of her clutter, Max decided it was high time to take control of a situation that had overwhelmed her over many years. Self-described as someone who is afraid of change - she just doesn't like it; she fears it - she had also recognized that copious clutter got in the way of her happiness, as well as blocked her way to the bathroom.

So on that first November day, Max chose ten things to clear from her space from the most benign, least painful spot - a kitchen drawer. She picked items from that drawer that she knew had no meaning in her life: four wooden spoons, a vintage tea saucer missing its matching tea-cup, two full boxes of coffee filters for a coffee maker she didn't own, a baggie with old refrigerator magnets, and two kitchen tools that she was not able to identify. Max put the ten things into her car and drove to the nearest donation center.

On November 2, Max did it again. And again and again and again. Between November 1st and March 31st, Max Wong cleared approximately 1500 unwanted and unused items from her house. On that last day of March, she said, "I walked into my house that day and noticed that things were noticeably clearer." Thirteen years later, Max continues to remove ten things per day.

When she began clearing the path of clutter and chaos, Max chose those random items that lacked an emotional hold over her heart or mind. She was able to trash or donate old pens and pencils, pots and pans, flatware and dusty candles missing their wicks. Business cards from people she didn't remember, books she never really intended to read, and a variety of other household items and knick-knacks made their way out the door at a relatively clipped and easy rate. She made up some rules along the way:

- She wouldn't go to bed unless she cleared ten items before 11:59 PM each day;
- The clearing "didn't count" unless the items actually left her space;
- She wouldn't count those items easily identified as trash (e.g., empty food containers, used Q-tips).

In her first ten-item clearing, Max could have counted each individual magnet in the baggie but she decided that since they were all encased in one-bag, she'd count as one item. Her rules. As the "easy stuff" departed her space, she soon understood that she would also have to start making some hard decisions about other stuff. Over time she developed additional ideas and questions to help her clear her space in more thoughtful ways and became "super hyper aware" of what was coming into her life and what would eventually go out:

- What is the shelf life of this object in my life?
- How will this item eventually leave my life?
- Does self-reliance mean that I need ready access to every tool that I know how to use (or not!)?

102

And she embraced the process of downward thinking by asking questions about each item she considered letting go:

- Do I need it? If yes, what is the scenario to emerge for me to use it?
- If I can't see an *immediate* need and let it go now, what kind of work will I have to do in order to bring a similar item back into my life?
- If I no longer have the item, do I have something else I can replace it with? Can I borrow from someone?
- Does the cost of this item (actual or emotional) outweigh my desire for a cleared path?

The art of letting go is discussed earlier in this book. Clearing just ten things a day gives structure to your desire for cleared space, it refines the practice of letting go. Making a commitment to ten things - a day, week, or month - provides a structured, thoughtful, and progress-oriented result. Each day you that put "clear just ten" into practice, brings you that much closer to your desired goal. Max told me, "In the 13 years I've been doing this, I honestly don't remember what I've gotten rid of."

If you can develop the attitude that your needs are always met because you can be flexible to the variety of ways in which they can be met, then you are truly on your way toward your vision for a cleared space.

Thirteen years later, Max maintains her decision to clear ten things a day, and said, "Sometimes you just get desperate and pull a bunch of jelly packets." As you read this you may be thinking, "Holy cow! That Max Wong must have had TONS of stuff to start and if she's still got stuff, well then... I'm just not that bad!" To which I respond... First, clutter is not a moral issue. There is no "good" or "bad" clutter - it's really just stuff. Second, we are human and we constantly bring all manner of things into our homes and cars, and every environment which we inhabit. We may use something once and then never again. We may pass by an object in the living room that we've passed by 100 times, but at that moment we recognized that the item had out-lived their usefulness. Most people who would walk into Max Wong's house would describe her decor as minimalist. The reality is that stuff will continue to make its way into our lives for the rest of our lives. We have to determine for ourselves what counts as clutter. What gets in the way of your desire for a peaceful and chaos-free life? Since clutter is such a personal matter, Max told me that she had to "re-train her eye" to what constitutes her version of clutter.

Max has taken her focus on de-cluttering into her community. She was donating dozens of items to local donation centers, and to friends who could really use what she was discarding. These daily drop-offs, akin to mobile garage sales (profiting by giving) gave her creative new ideas for letting go, making it easier to continue the process. In her neighborhood she often walked past crumbling concrete steps at the edge of an abandoned dirt lot. She began drop-ping off old sets of dishes and Corningware pots that had seen better days, or clothes and shoes, hotel soaps and shampoos. And just as quickly as these things arrived, they would be gone that night or the next day.

Dubbing the area the "Trading Post" the edge of the lot has become quite popular for other in-kind donations. "If I curb something and it's not gone the next day it's obviously trash, no one wants it, and I throw it away." She also hosts quarterly book and clothing exchanges with friends and people who live in the 'hood.

These community endeavors planted seeds in those who participated - about one's personal environment and places where they live. From clearing just ten to getting the entire neighborhood involved in clearing their own stuff, well, that's a lot of things getting back out into the world that others can use.

Clear Just 10, Then Do It Again:
A new approach to an old problem

Max Wong's desire for less clutter in her home and community inspired me to develop a new virtual community called *Clear Just 10, then Do it Again* where you commit to clearing just ten things a day. What you clear is up to you.

This is a program designed for the chronically cluttered and disorganized. Most people with a lot of clutter experience a lot of difficulty in dealing with it. As such, clearing clutter can often be a lonely, frustrating, and seemingly impossible endeavor; a lot of people give up before they even get started, and:

- You just don't know where to begin
- It feels too overwhelming to do anything about it
- Even when you clear your clutter it always seems to return
- Your place is too small
- You don't have places to put your stuff
- You don't make good use of your space
- You can't clear it alone and you're too ashamed to ask for help
- Clutter and disorganization have always been part of your life and you've resigned yourself to life amongst the rubble
  If any of these statements ring true then *Clear just 10 (then do it again)* is for you!

The premise: Make a commitment to clear ten things a day and report to our virtual community on your progress. It's up you; you're in control.

How it works:

- Consider joining our closed Facebook page and start meeting with like-minded people who are willing to make a commitment to changing and transforming their lives.
(https://www.facebook.com/groups/clearjust10/?ref=br_tf)

- At the FB page, I regularly post interesting and challenging questions and ideas about our relationship to our cluttered spaces.

- You will connect with other members of our community ready and willing to make a commitment to change.

- You can share your stories: about the stuff you are clearing, how you'll use your cleared space, about your progress and about your challenges.

- Post pictures about what's heading out the door!

- Support each other!

- Be accountable to your goals to *Clear Just 10 (then do it again!)!*

MAINTAIN A CLEAR AND UNCLUTTERED SPACE

The dictionary (www.dictionary.com) says *maintain* means to keep in existence or continuance, to preserve or retain, to keep in an appropriate condition, operation or force, keep unimpaired, to maintain order, and to keep in a specified state or position. This definition indicates that to *maintain* is to keep the *status quo*. I want to caution you away from that. What we're doing here is to really think outside the box, to push the envelope of how we're thinking about our stuff, our environment, and our relationships to things that we've kept because we believe they have meaning or potential in our life. By maintaining that thinking, you'll *never* un-clutter!

Companies hire me to design what I call *Clear the Path Day*. I meet with employee before the event to talk with them about the process of de-cluttering. Some people, of course, have a tremendous amount of clarity when it comes to what they need to do in their workspace, and there are others who simply are clueless. They just don't know where to start. So for *Clear the Path Day*, the office shuts down and all phones as much as possible are sent to voicemail. The manager orders food and we have fun music. Recycle containers are brought in and distributed throughout the work place. We dig in and start clearing the path. I walk around to each cubicle to see what people are doing, and how they are de-cluttering their spaces. Sometimes I'll walk by one cubicle to hear someone say, "Great! We've finally got time to get this work done." At another cubicle someone just looks at me with a blank stare and say, "I don't know what to do." I spend one-on-one time with that person. After I get everyone started, I'll check in with them throughout the day. The folks who are able to make sense of their mess are left to their own devices.

It does so much for morale as people create a heck of a lot more space in the workplace. It is a fun win-win for all involved. In addition, the managers look like they really understand that the employees need to have the dedicated time to get things cleared up.

The company managers invested a great deal of resources to clear the path with the goal of maintaining the newly uncluttered spaces. Don't you wish you could do that in your workplace? How about in your home?

I'm reframing the definition of *maintain* to your new state, this new status that you have developed about your relationship with your stuff. But before I begin, I want you to review what we've already done, that is, creating positive affirmations and designing your plan to clear your space.

Write your vision, your reason why you want to have clear space. Having that vision, the words and message, in front of you will be a reminder 24/7 about why this work is important to you. While your vision may change over time, having it in writing goes a long way to keep you focused.

Assignment:

What is your vision? Write it here.

Break the work into small sections. Professional Organizers call this chunking, breaking it down into small pieces. In one of my workshops, a client talked about being so over-whelmed with how much there was to do. I made a simple suggestion: do it one drawer at a time. I could see the light bulb go off over her head. It was not something she had considered. All she could see was the big-picture mess be-fore her. We get so caught up in how much there is to do that we find it very difficult to look at it in tiny bite-sized pieces, the little morsels to be devoured one at a time.

Assignment:

Break down your project here. Think of the smallest spaces such as a drawer or a shelf, then begin:

_____
_____
_____
_____
_____
_____
_____
_____
_____
_____
_____
_____
_____
_____

In order to maintain this, I'll share some thoughts about how you may work on your projects and then *maintain* a clutter-free body, mind, spirit, and space. Let's begin.

One way to maintain this is to keep it in your consciousness. It's a daily activity. We talked about writing down your reasons and your goals for de-cluttering. Each time you walk into a space, think about one little thing you can do to make it better. Complete projects over a week's period of time, or even a couple of months, but maintain as a daily activity. Keep your goals in front of you.

Assignment:

Why did you choose this particular time in your life to do this work? What is it about a clutter-free or simplistic life that is attractive to you?

_____

—_____

_____

_____

_____

_____

_____

_____

_____

_____

_____

_____

_____

Writing is often a precursor to commitment. Place it where you'll see it on a regular basis, somewhere where you look everyday. It could be the bathroom, the kitchen, next to your bed, wherever you will automatically see it.

Notes to myself:

_____

_____

_____

_____

_____

_____

_____

_____

_____

_____

_____

_____

_____

_____

_____

_____

_____

_____

_____

_____

_____

_____

_____

_____

MAINTAIN:
A NEW WAY OF THINKING AND DOING

M: Mind Mapping

A great strategy for maintaining as a daily activity is mind mapping. I love this stuff! I did one when I bought my house and when I started A Clear Path. I helped a friend do one because she was having many health issues.

To create a mind map (also called a "vision board"), decide on a theme. In this case it would be a clutter-free environment or perhaps to rid yourself of clutter, however you want to phrase the theme.

Get a poster board from your local office supply store and cut it in half. In the middle of it, in block letters write "clutter-free life." Go through old magazines that you're going to be donating or recycling anyway and cut out words and images of what represents your vision.

When I started A Clear Path, my mind map included several pictures of pathways that were clear. I had a picture of a very comfortable bathrobe because I want comfort in my life. I included a globe because I want travel in my life, and I saw my Clear Path business as bringing these themes and desires into my life. I had a money symbol made of toys which represented for me that money is fun. However I was envisioning A Clear Path when I started, I cut out images to represent my thinking about it. I kept it on my bedroom closet door so that it was the first thing I saw when I opened my eyes and the last thing I saw at the end of my day. Keeping the visual in front of me all the time served as a constant reminder of what I was working towards. There are no rules to mind mapping. Google it. You'll see hundreds of examples.

A: Act

The first "A" in MAINTAIN is to Act. For example, open your mail when it arrives and act on each piece. Don't let it sit somewhere unopened, piling up. Don't bring it into your space unless it's going to have a home. Do it now, not later.

When you come across something in your space that doesn't serve you, remove it. Now that you have a very different mindset about what clutter is for you, this is now your new default. Walk around and identify what you don't need, and without thinking (or feeling) about it further, let it go. Remove it with to the trash or to the donation pile. Do this until it becomes habitual. If you maintain a strong consciousness around de-cluttering, less is going to come into your space and more will go out. You will find the balance of clear space while being around your lovely things without de-cluttering your life. *Acting* is an important component to how you're going to maintain this work.

I wrote an article about having to let go of the books and papers from my doctoral library. I donated or gave away hundreds of books because they were no longer serving me.

Did you know that the average person reads about two books a month. That's 24 books a year! So starting at the age of eight until the age of 88, the average person will read approximately 1,920 books in her or his lifetime!

That's a lot of books! But some people have more books and magazines than they could possibly read in their life-time. If you do, let them go. If you have issues with books and magazines, the public library is your best friend. I cov-et my library card. If I hear about something, I go online and I order it through the public library. It doesn't even matter when it's coming because I always have something that I can read. And it's a pleasant surprise when something I ordered, something that's been in the queue for several weeks or months, suddenly is available! I have a new book ready for me to pick up. It's like getting a gift. And then I can give it back when I'm finished, or renew it if I'm not. I just don't have book clutter anymore. I'm in love with my public library! If you can afford an electronic reader, fall in love with that, too!

I: Inform

Inform others is next. Ask gift givers for restaurant gift cards, or encourage the giver to donate in your name to a favorite charity rather than bring an extra item into your space. Tell people close to you of your desire to minimize. If you need something from them, you'll ask. Often, people in their own de-cluttering process will pass their clutter along to a family member thinking that they may want the item. Most folks are polite and accept it. My question is always this: Is the de-clutterer just trying to keep from making a final decision, thereby forcing another family member to decide the final disposition of the item?

Have conversations with people to whom you're close to let them know that you're on this new path for a de-cluttered life. It may help keep things at bay and it will allow you to maintain your newly-de-cluttered life. Learn to release the negative feelings about yourself, your home, your life, and to thoughts that don't advance your higher purpose. Release the people in your life who are not there for your highest good.

People, too!? Yes! I call that the two-legged clutter. Sometimes we have people in our life who just aren't serving us. I personally choose to be around people that are uplifting and elevating. It's very hard for me to be in the presence of negative people. They're always complaining or they feel like everybody's out to get them or they're not getting enough of x, y and z, or they hate their boss and they're not taking any steps to create a different situation for themselves. Two-legged clutter will bring us down. I'm going to encourage you to release the people from your life who bring you down. Some people may say, "Oh you don't have that much clutter. You're not that bad." They're not walking in your shoes. They don't know how you feel about what the clutter is doing to you. So saying no to negativity, to ideas that aren't advancing your higher good, and the people who aren't supporting what it is that you want to achieve and accomplish, or who are just bummers, the Debbie-downers, are not serving you in any way. Just say no! Begin to make that a new habit.

N: Nurture Yourself!

Nurture yourself. Pat yourself on the back frequently. Create rewards for meeting your short-term goals of clearing an area. Take yourself out to a nice dinner, or if you decluttered on a Saturday afternoon, make the end of your day a great walk or go bowling or just do something you enjoy. I recently started playing golf and I love it. I'm having so much fun learning how to play, and now it's on my calendar. Whenever I see an open space of time, I have the word *golf* to consider. Should I have a big chunk of free time, I fill that time with this work that I love, no questions asked, but I realized I needed to incorporate fun into my life, and golf just seems to be the thing that has chosen me or I've chosen it to do. Fun is a way of self-nurturing and making sure that you stay clear in body, mind and spirit. I want my headspace clear so that I may continue doing the work that I enjoy and makes me happy.

Reward yourself, nurture yourself, find that balance. I know many people work full-time and are very tired at the end of the day, and the clutter has kept them from enjoying life. I'm working with a couple who have been together for over 20 years. Their biggest fight is about their massive clutter. They're golf pros and they love being outdoors. They love playing the game and yet they don't have time to play because they feel trapped into having to clear this room or the other, and it doesn't get done. They brought me in to help clear their path. Their goal was to get back out and play together again. I had them write that and put it on the refrigerator and on their bathroom mirrors. They have their goals front and center. But they couldn't do it by themselves. They brought me in and I was able to work with them, encourage them, until they felt they had succeeded with their de-cluttering project. Now they spend their time playing golf with friends rather than stressing about the mess in their house.

T: Trust

Trust that the process will unfold as it should. Trust that there is nothing standing in the way of your achieving your goals. Trust that your choices - of what to keep, toss, and donate - are perfect, right, and good. Trust that the only thing keeping you from realizing your goals is, well, you! Trust that no matter how you approach each cluttered space, that you will do the right thing. Trust in the power of your mind, heart, and body. Trust in this axiom: Conceive, Believe, Achieve.

A: Advance

The next word is *advance*. Keep the momentum going. Take baby steps if you need to, but keep moving forward. You want to pass along your newfound tools to help your friends and family members in similar situations, and advance the notion that you can be cleared of clutter.

Often, de-cluttering is a very lonely process. I encourage people to find a friend who also has clutter, somebody you're close to who is non-judgmental, and trade off helping each other. Make it a project. Get on each other's calendar. Mutual support. You want somebody who can say, "Honey, that never looked good on you anyway so let it go," and that you won't take offense. Of course, you want someone to be loving and gentle and kind, as you are with them. If something is really challenging for you, and you're avoiding de-cluttering, you may want to have someone there to act as a body buddy. They may come over to your space and work on something else while you are going through your paper files.

The buddy system works really well for folks who procrastinate and don't want to tackle a particular project. I know an organizer who has severe ADD, and she works great with her clients. When it comes to tackling her own stuff, she does really well when a friend comes over and just sits in the room while she takes care of a pile of papers that she's been avoiding.

Another friend had a head filled with psychic debris and she was constantly degrading herself that she wasn't good enough or smart enough. She didn't even realize how often she was putting herself down. I told her that I'd love to help her get away from that mindset. She agreed and allowed me to call her on her head trash. When I heard something come out of her mouth, I'd say "Wow, you're doing it again. You just said X. Let's see how we can replace it with something else." It was startling to her because she did not realize how often she was putting herself down.

I: Invest

Invest in your decision to un-clutter by telling those whom you trust, and who you believe will support the process, about your desire for a cleared path. Invest in yourself: work with a professional organizer, life coach, and/or therapist, to get you started, help you through rough patches, or to otherwise add to your support team. Invest with a friend: help a friend de-clutter their space and let your friend return the favor. Invest in the vision you are creating for your de-cluttered space is sacred - build on it, be creative, allow yourself to envision how your new space will look, sound, and feel like.

N: Never

The final N stands for Never...as in Never give up! If you've got a big mess, give yourself a year or two to clear it; nothing has to happen overnight. This work, after all, is a process and you did not manage to acquire your clutter overnight so know that you don't have to make the big changes in a week! Create your mind map, enlist the help of a friend or professional, write the plan of action (which room or area first, next, etc). Never stop believing in your ability to get through the really tough decisions. And never, never, never stop believing in YOU!

CONCLUSION

Psychic debris and crowded closets are acquired habits. Just as you brought the clutter into your space, you are now giving yourself permission to let it leave your space. And while it is often the case that head trash can be the result of many things: childhood messages, negative friends, or low self-esteem - myriad tools are available to help clear the head space for a more productive life.

Finding and reading this book should tell you something: you recognize that you have a problem and you haven't given up on yourself!! These are really good things to know about yourself. Take advantage of everything that is available to ensure your success. Get a good sleep the night before your project, and be sure to eat your Wheaties on the day of your project. If you have ADHD or just feel a little squirrely, set a timer. Ask a friend to help. Play awesome music and dance your way through the de-cluttering process. Create rituals to help you let go. One client with whom I've had the privilege of working with used to have a hard time with the letting go process. Now she takes pictures of the stuff she used to value but is now willing and able to let go to the universe. I think it's such an awesome idea. Bottom line: Do what ever you can think of to ensure your success.

I have faith in you.

SONGS IN THE KEY OF REGINA
FROM
DR. REGINA'S ORGANIZER SONG BOOK

**The Organizer Song
(to the tune of "My Favorite Things")**

I love your clutter oh let me get at it!
Sorting and grouping, I'm nearly an addict.
Paper clips, tsotchkies, and binders with rings,
These are a few of my favorite things.

Bumm-dabada-bumm-dabada
Bumm-dabada-bumm-dabada

Miles of files and 8-tracks and cables.
'Containerize this! Oh you'll love it with labels!
Organized kitchens, and closets and beads.
Call us we'll help with your de-clutter needs!

Use a timer!
Think of SMART Goals!
Fold it this way and you'll see...
Just Clear the Path now, don't delay, this is how...
And soon you be ...
Relieved!

Defining Clarity
(to the tune of Defying Gravity)

Something has changed within me
Some things are not the same.
I'm through with holding on to things
that only cause me pain!

I'll clear my path of clutter
Tossing things that I don't need.
I'm ready to let go now, declare myself as FREE!

It's time to try defining CLARITY
I think I'll try defining CLARITY
Kiss this goodbye, I'm defining CLARITY
A Clear Path showed me how!

Imagine No Clutter
(sing to the tune of Imagine)

Imagine there's no clutter;
It isn't hard to do
No need for too much;
A little bit is cool.
Imagine kitchen counters with just a bowl of fruit - oo oo...

Doncha Think It's Sexy
(to the tune of "Do Ya Think I'm Sexy)

Doncha think it's sexy and I paid good money,
Now you tell me let it go?
No I've never used it, but I'm sure I'll need it
Please don't make me let it go!

Crazy Clutter
(to the tune of Crazy)
Crazy, this clutter is making me crazy!
And I'm crazy - this chaos is making me blue.
And I know, I want to take time to attack it;
But then really, I don't have a clue what do!

Let it Go
(to the tune of Let it Snow)

Oh the clutter inside is frightful
And. my dear, it's not delightful
So let's give it the old heave-ho!
Let it go, let it go, let it go!

References

Stephen Covey, Time Management Matrix.
http://www.mindtools.com/pages/article/newHTE_91.htm

Dictionary. http://dictionary.reference.com/

Melva Green and Lauren Rosenfeld, *Breathing Room: Open Your Heart by Decluttering your Home* Atria Books/Beyond Words, 2014.

Louise Hay, *You Can Heal Your Life* Hay House, Inc., 1984. http://www.hayhouse.com/details.php?id=267

Napoleon Hill, *Think & Grow Rich* Wilshire Book Co., 1966. http://www.naphill.org/

Institute for Challenging Disorganization
http://www.challengingdisorganization.org/

Judith Kolberg, *Getting Organized in the Era of Endless,* Squall Press, 2013.

Judith Kolberg, *Conquering Chronic Disorganization* 2d ed., Squall Press, 2007.

Judith Kolberg and Kathleen Nadeau, Ph.D. *ADD-Friendly Ways to Organize Your Life.* Routledge/Taylor & Francis Group, 2002.

Regina F. Lark, Ph.D., CPO,® CPO-CD®. *Psychic Debris, Crowded Closets: The Relationship Between the Stuff in Your Head and What's Under your Bed.* 2d ed., Purple Distincions, 2014.

Lanna Nakone, M.A. *Organizing for your Brain Type.* St. Martin's Press, 2005.

Sari Solden. *Women with Attention Deficit Disorder: Embrace your Difference and Transform your Life.* Underwood Books, 205.

Michael Tompkins and Tamara Hartl. *Digging Out: Helping Your Loved Ones Manage Clutter, Hoarding, and Compulsive Acquiring.* New Harbinger Publications, 2009.

Kate Varness, CPO-CD,® ed., *The ICD Guide to Challenging Disorganization.* Institute for Challenging Disorganization, 2012.

Max Wong blogs, http://www.myromanapartment.com/ http://www.wisebread.com/max-wong.

ABOUT THE AUTHOR

Dr. Regina Lark is founder and president of *A Clear Path: Professional Organizing for Home, Work, Life*. As a Certified Professional Organizer in Chronic Disorganization (CPO-CD) she specializes in working with people with chronic disorganization, ADHD, hoarding disorders, as well as the folks with way too much stuff!

Regina, a Certified Professional Organizer, serves as President of the Board of Directors for NAPO-Los Angeles. She is a speaker and trainer on issues ranging from hoarding to time management. Regina's first book, *Psychic Debris, Crowded Closets: The Relationship between the Stuff in your Head and What's Under your Bed* (Purple Books Publishing), was released in 2013. Her second book, *Before the Big O: Professional Organizers Talk about Life before Organizing* was published 2014.

Regina ran for the office of Lt. Governor in California in 1998, and a year later completed her Ph.D. in history from the University of Southern California. For fun, she teaches U.S. History at Los Angeles Pierce College.

Made in the USA
San Bernardino, CA
04 August 2016